I0457267

THE FIVE DRIVERS
OF SUCCESS

Identify and Eliminate the Limiters
that Are Preventing You from
Achieving Your Best Career...and Life.

BY MIKE ACKER

Copyright ©2023, Mike Acker

All rights reserved. No part of this publication may be reproduced, distributed, or transmitted in any form or by any means, including photocopying, recording, or other electronic or mechanical methods, without the prior written permission of the publisher, except in the case of brief quotations embodied in reviews and certain other non-commercial uses permitted by copyright law.

Some names and identifying details have been changed to protect the privacy of individuals.

https://www.advantage-publishing.com

To contact, please e-mail: contact@mikeacker.com

TABLE OF CONTENTS

INTRODUCTION:

What's Limiting You?

Although a bottle of "Pappy Van Winkle's Family Reserve 23 Year Old" bourbon lists at $300, its popularity and limited availability causes it to sell for as much as $9,000. I don't think any whiskey is worth $500 a shot, but plenty of people disagree.

Let's say that you somehow win a barrel of Pappy's 23. With a capacity of two hundred and sixty-six bottles, you're looking at over $2,000,000 worth of whiskey!

Now, imagine you go to pick it up from the distiller, and discover one of the staves (the barrel's wooden "planks") has broken about halfway down and twenty-five gallons of liquid gold has been lost down the drain...

Hold that thought for a moment and feel the high cost of that needless waste.

LIMITS VS. LEAKS

Every one of us faces various personal limits that we must be content with. You'll never be as inspirational as Dr. Martin Luther King Jr., as smart as Einstein, or as fast as Kenyan marathoner Eliud Kipchoge. Think of these limits as representing the overall capacity of your "barrel."

As an executive coach who has worked with high-profile clients, spoken to over 10,000 people, been mentored by highly skilled professionals, read countless books (and written many of my own), and made self-examination a way of life, I've discovered that most people's barrels—mine included—are far bigger than they realize.

> *Most people's barrels are far bigger than they realize.*

Back to the leaking barrel of Pappy's 23... It's designed to hold fifty-three gallons, but that doesn't matter. Nor do the thirty-one staves that go all the way to the top. It's the one broken stave that limits the barrel's actual capacity.

Over the past twenty-four years, I've worked with eager and talented young people looking for the quickest way to the top. I've worked with frustrated professionals who didn't understand why they plateaued or kept getting passed up by less qualified coworkers. I've worked with discouraged executives who wondered if they'd come up against the "Peter Principle" ("members of a hierarchy are promoted until they reach the level at which they are no longer competent") and were incapable of significant improvement.

These experiences have shown me that there isn't just one Success Limiter or one silver bullet that can fix anyone, let alone everyone. Instead, I've realized there are *five* core competencies which everyone must develop continually. These are the five drivers of success. None of them are revolutionary, but neither are any of them optional.

Here is the most important principle of this entire book: Your biggest limitation isn't your barrel's capacity, but the shortest Success Stave. *That* is what is preventing you from realizing your greatest possible success—not just in your career but also in relationships, finances, and personal growth.

Your biggest limitation isn't your barrel's capacity, but your shortest Success Stave.

That's the bad news.

The good news is that, unlike your total capacity, each of these five drivers of success can be fixed.

Maybe you started strong but have stalled out. Maybe you've tried everything but still don't know why you can't get ahead. Maybe you're just starting out and you want to chart the best path forward (great for you—that's smart thinking). Whatever the case, addressing these five Success Limiters will allow you to discover and attain your true potential.

I promise you, your barrel is bigger than you think.

SUCCESS LIMITERS VS. WEAKNESSES

Early in my career, I took the CliftonStrengths assessment, and it changed how I thought about professional development. More than just identifying my strengths, I learned not to waste energy on improving my weaknesses (those areas where I'll never be better than "mediocre") and instead, pour that effort into the areas I can truly excel in.

Success Limiters are very different from weaknesses. Weaknesses should be tolerated and, if possible, outsourced to others, but Success Limiters can only be dealt with by you. Think of them like personal hygiene—I can hire people to make up for my weakness in administrative skills but not to make up for not showering or wearing deodorant.

Do you see what I'm saying? As you read through the five Success Limiters below, your gut response to at least one of them will be, "Yeah, X just isn't my forte." And *that* is what is limiting your success.

While your strengths and weaknesses will determine *how* you address each of the Success Limiters, the only way to discover your actual capacity is by achieving your personal best in each of these areas. So, sorry (but not really) for taking away your excuses. Again, that's the bad news.

Here's more good news:

Very few people are willing to tackle all five Success Limiters. Remember what makes the Pappy's 23 so valuable? Rarity. If you're willing to push past your excuses, you'll be unstoppable and will quietly start passing up seemingly more talented people. Even if their capacity is theoretically greater than yours, having five Success Staves that go all the way to the top will beat them out.

If you're willing to push past your excuses, you'll be unstoppable.

THE BIG FIVE

Here are the five Success Limiters that are at the root of every disappointing story I've come across:

1. Ignorance (often mixed with arrogance)

2. Inexperience

3. Poor communication skills

4. Inability to work with others

5. Apathy

Conversely, here are the five drivers of success, aka the five Success Staves. As I said, there's nothing revolutionary here (but I promise to give surprising insights on each):

1. Knowledge: How much *relevant* information do you possess?

2. Experience: How proficient are you in your field?

3. Communication: How well can you convey yourself and understand others?

4. Emotional Intelligence: How clearly do you understand yourself and "play well with others"?

5. Drive: How much are you willing to sacrifice to achieve your goals?

Before we continue, rank yourself on each of these five Success Staves, from tallest to shortest, and explain your answer.

Note: Even if you typically ignore discussion questions, I'd encourage you to at least read and reflect on them as you go through this book—they are vital for the assessment and repair of your Success Staves.

1. Knowledge

   _____

   _____

2. Experience

   _____

   _____

3. Communication

   _____

   _____

4. Emotional Intelligence

   _____

   _____

5. Drive

   _____

   _____

Which one of the five Success Limiters do you most frequently excuse as a "weakness"? (Ignorance, Inexperience, Poor communication skills, Inability to work with others, Apathy.)

_____

_____

_____

_____

Final question: How do you think your life would look if all these Success Staves were fixed and you were operating at your true capacity?

_____

_____

_____

_____

_____

_____

_____

Are you ready to get started? Then turn the page, because the sooner you fix your Success Staves, the quicker your barrel will fill up!

CHAPTER 1:

Knowledge

The younger you are, the easier it is to equate knowledge with formal education. That's not surprising—it's been your entire focus since preschool. Parents start pushing college shortly after kindergarten graduation. Keeping your GPA up has been objective #1. Hiring decisions are frequently based on nothing more than your alma mater.

Formal education has a certain value. It demonstrates you have the discipline to complete a degree and (hopefully) will give you the information you need to enter your field. However, a degree doesn't guarantee success and the lack of one doesn't doom you.

A degree doesn't guarantee success and the lack of one doesn't doom you.

Take Chandler Bolt for example. If you've ever googled "self-publish my book," you've likely seen ads for his Self-Publishing School. It was this well-developed system that helped me write, publish, and promote my first book (more on that later).

In 2022, he was recognized as one of *Forbes* "30 Under 30 in Education" but his *Forbes'* profile states (and I quote), "Education: Drop Out, College of Charleston."[1] As funny as that is, it's not quite an accurate description of Bolt. He's extremely well educated, just not through the traditional route. He's an avid reader who has studied nearly every major business book ever printed and has been mentored by many successful leaders and entrepreneurs. So, while Bolt doesn't have a degree, he's actively pursued knowledge and has tons of experience. He is also a great communicator, exudes emotional intelligence, and is incredibly driven.

My point isn't "you don't need an education." Whether or not you need a degree or certification will be determined by your situation and career path. But the intentional and systematic accumulation of knowledge (i.e., education) is a non-negotiable driver of success.

To be clear, I'm not talking about knowledge in general. Killing it at "Trivia Nite" isn't a good predictor of success but being an authority in your

---

[1] https://www.forbes.com/profile/chandler-bolt/?sh=2b57ab17d962

field is. Every profession and pursuit requires you to know certain things. Whether you're a doctor, bartender, writer, CEO, or coder, there is information that you absolutely need to know and not having it will absolutely hold you back.

OBSTACLES TO KNOWLEDGE

What causes people to come up short on knowledge?

- Some are too proud to admit that they don't know everything (even to themselves).
- Some are afraid of learning—ignorance feels safer.
- Some just aren't willing to do the work.

Pride, fear, and laziness are all common barriers to knowledge; however, if you're reading this book and have already experienced some level of success, then those may not be your biggest obstacles. In my experience, the most underestimated obstacle to fixing this Success Limiter is…

Boredom.

Surprised? Don't be. Maybe boredom has cost you more than you realize—it almost cost me my success as an executive and communication coach.

I effectively started coaching in my early 20s, working with other students in my college's nationally ranked debate team. I'd been deeply impacted by our program and was excited to share what I'd gained. Later, as an executive director, I learned a lot about business principles and had the opportunity to mentor other entrepreneurs. It was both fun and personally gratifying—less work than a hobby that I sometimes got paid for. As I transitioned into the business world, people began approaching me for formal coaching and it ceased to be a hobby and became a job. So, I leaned into it and really got to work, developing systems that made a difference in people's lives.

Coaching was still incredibly rewarding, but my systems were almost too effective. Without a daily challenge, I started to get bored by the day-in and day-out of the program. Having studied communication and leadership so much, I began to develop a "been there, done that attitude." One of the strengths my CliftonStrengths assessment showed is Activator, which means I love starting things, so I experimented with subcontracting out the coaching and looked for my next challenge. Fortunately, various circumstances forced me to reengage the coaching. That, in turn, drove me to dive in deeper, leading to a breakthrough and a whole new level of understanding about communication and coaching—it turns out I didn't know everything (and still don't)! It was that breakthrough that led to my benchmark book, *Speak with Confidence*, and a rediscovery of my passion.

Does this sound at all familiar to you? Have you grown bored in your current position? Keep reading to learn more about breaking through what I call the "Boredom Barrier."

THREE LEVELS OF KNOWLEDGE

As a public speaker and coach of other speakers, I've discovered that there are three levels of knowledge:

1. Inspiration

2. Familiarity

3. Understanding

The first level is like a high school junior whose world is rocked when he reads Maya Angelou's words, "You alone are enough. You have nothing to prove to anybody."

The second is when, after much self-reflection, he chooses to use that quote to encourage others in his valedictorian speech.

The third is when Maya herself says them after a lifetime of living them. It's the same words but her depth of experience embodies them in a way that changes everything.

Think about when you first got interested in your field. Something probably inspired you and drew you beyond mere curiosity and you committed yourself. As you kept learning new aspects, it continued to hold your interest. But at some point, the novelty wore off and the "been there, done that" attitude hit you, creating an illusion of mastery. It can be graphed like this:

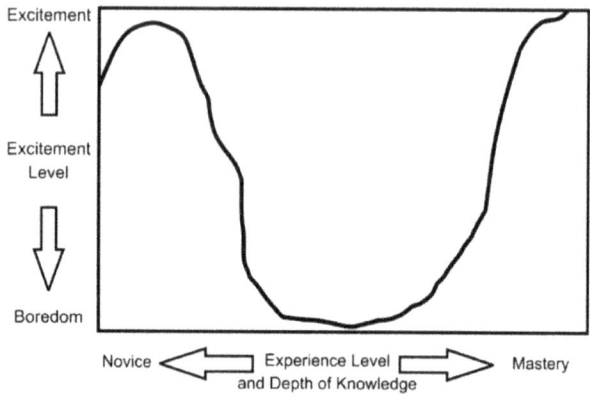

PUSHING PAST FAMILIARITY

It's easy to go from inspiration to familiarity—just study it a couple times, think about it a little bit, and start teaching it to others. Congratulations, you're now familiar with the concept. But going from familiarity to genuine understanding and being an expert is a long, arduous journey. I like to say that familiarity has ten sub-levels. These aren't literally ranks you can check off, like saying, "I'm a seventh-degree coder." It means that there's a process to pushing past the Boredom Barrier.

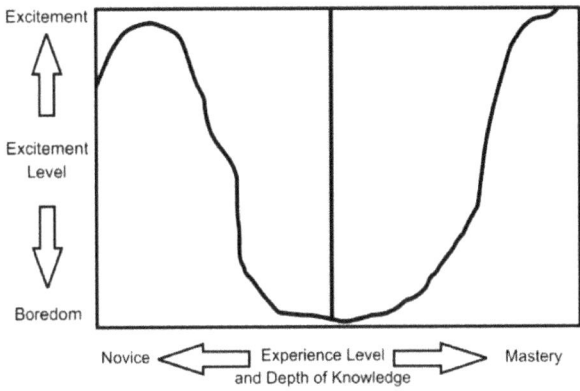

I believe it's impossible to gain understanding without pushing past the lull in excitement, i.e., the Boredom Barrier. It's kind of like transitioning from dating into a deep relationship. Dating is exciting, but that excitement naturally wanes as the relationship deepens (that's when you discover if there is more to it than hormones.) Taylor and I have been married for thirteen years now, and we've gone through that lull (and our share of struggles) and are growing in our excitement—but now with a greater depth and understanding of each other.

It's impossible to gain understanding without pushing past the lull in excitement.

A little while back, I was in Washington, DC training a group of professionals on how to develop their "executive presence." One of the participants, a behavioral scientist, observed that the above pattern mimicked the Dunning–Kruger effect, which basically says people with a modicum of ability or expertise in an area tend to overestimate their knowledge and people with high expertise tend to underestimate it. In other words, if you think you know it all—and are starting to get bored—it only proves how little you know!

The Dunning–Kruger effect, in turn, prevents you from learning more. I once had two people working under me. They were in roughly the same position, same age, and at similar levels of familiarity with the job. The first guy would ask me a question. In the process of answering it, I'd inadvertently say things he already knew. But he was humble (and secure) enough to just nod along with interest. As a result, I'd continue talking and give him a more well-rounded answer. He'd have an "Aha!" moment and progress to a deeper level of familiarity.

The second guy, however, seemed worried I was underestimating him and would start injecting things like, "Yeah, I know…" and "No, I got that…" As a result, I lost interest in helping him with his problem and kept my feedback short.

One day, I stopped him. "You asked me a question so you could learn something, right? But you're acting like you've heard it all. Sure, you're familiar with what I'm saying, but that's keeping you from really listening. Understand, you'll never hear what you need to know until you listen to what you already know."

You'll never hear what you need to know until you listen to what you already know.

GIVING UP TOO SOON

I'm convinced many people change jobs when they should be doubling down. If I would've given up coaching because of boredom, I wouldn't have created my "framework for confidence," had my seminal book published by a well-respected publisher, or become a TEDx speaker.

When you think you know it all... go deeper.

When you get bored... go deeper.

When you daydream about switching careers... go deeper.

Pushing past the Boredom Barrier takes work. You'll have to create new motivational systems to make up for the lack of excitement. You may need to take classes on your own dime or read books in your free time. But that's very good news. Why? Because 80% of people won't do it. If you're willing to put in the hours and invest your years, you'll eliminate this

Success Limiter and set yourself up for greater success—and be one of the few who have.

WHEN TO STOP

Before we proceed, there's an important caveat. In the same way that few people should marry their first crush, not everyone should stay at their first job, or maybe even their second, third, or fourth.

When I was 21, I decided to get out of the college library and get a roofing job to experience some good, old-fashioned manual labor. I didn't really enjoy it when I began but knew that starting anything is tough. Two weeks later, after I'd gotten the hang of it, I still hated roofing. That was a good sign roofs weren't my calling!

Every job provides an opportunity to learn something, and many workplaces can be fun (and even pay well). That doesn't guarantee they're your path to success though. How do you know when to call it quits and when to push through the Boredom Barrier? There's no single answer but, if you're feeling restless, here are some questions to ask yourself:

- Does the job align with your strengths?

- Did you ever have an "inspiration stage"?

- Do you believe you're doing something valuable?

- Are your best days the ones where you go home tired but happy?

- Would you still enjoy doing the same basic work at a different place and/or with different people?

BE THE EXPERT

As I said before, every profession has a minimum amount of knowledge needed to do the job, but minimum does not equal success. If you're killing it in each of the four other Success Drivers but are still stuck, this might be your Success Limiter. Truly successful people are *experts* in their field and that should be your goal.

Truly successful people are experts in their field and that should be your goal.

Being an expert means, first of all, having a depth of knowledge—knowing more of the relevant facts than 90% of the people in your field and probably more than 100% of the people in your organization. But more important than facts is having a deep understanding. This moves from "who, what, where" to "why and how" and having the ability to apply your knowledge in divergent ways. It also means being able to communicate what you know to others effectively (Success Stave #3). Finally (and this should go without saying), being an expert is not a destination or title but a lifetime journey of curiosity and learning.

SELF-ASSESSMENT

Where would you put yourself on the following graph, noting both your knowledge and excitement level? Mark it with the word "me."

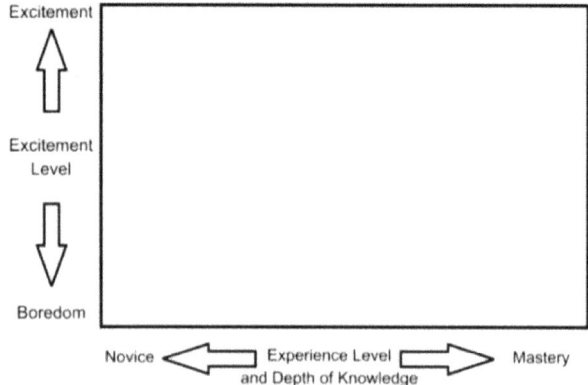

Who in your organization or personal circles is the most knowledgeable in your field? Mark that person's location with his/her name. Now, do the same for the least knowledgeable person.

Based on that information, give yourself an "expert rating," expressed using school-styled grades (from "A" to "F").

Now we need to compensate for the Dunning-Kruger effect. If you aren't already familiar with it, spend some time researching before answering these questions:

Why can you trust your "expert rating"? What objective evidence can you offer?

How difficult is it for you to admit when you're wrong or don't know something? Are you willing to ask for advice from a person instead of just searching the internet?

Based on your reading and answers to the last two questions, do you need to adjust your "expert rating" up or down?

_____

Looking again at your excitement level, do you think the Boredom Barrier is in your future, present, or past? Why?

_____

_____

If you're facing it now or will soon, how do you plan on overcoming it?

_____

_____

_____

_____

CHAPTER 2:

Experience

I'll never forget this one LinkedIn message. A recruiter for one of America's biggest companies reached out to me because they'd seen my books and were impressed with my work. Now they were asking me to apply for a full-time position as a speaking coach to their c-suite executives.

At first, I wondered if the message was real but quickly established its validity. The second interview—with the guy who would be my boss— went *really* well and he started talking as if I was already hired. Start date? In six weeks. Salary? Generous. Was I willing to travel to places like Tokyo, Madrid, and Stockholm to coach "my" team? Sure... If you make me...

After a few days, I received their conclusion. Although they didn't have any problems with me or my material, they needed someone who had more c-suite experience at the Fortune 100 level than I had at the time. I was disappointed, of course, but I understood. Afterall, sometimes there's simply no substitute for experience.

10,000 HOURS

It doesn't matter if we're talking about an athlete, musician, or bartender—there's something about watching a master at his/her craft.

In his book, *Outliers: The Story of Success*, Malcolm Gladwell introduced the "10,000 Hour Rule." According to his theory, that's the amount of practice required to gain complete proficiency in any given field. In reality, it's more of a rule of thumb than an actual rule because the amount of time varies from one person to another and from field to field—a kazoo will take less time to master than a cello (but there are kazoo virtuosos[2]).

My point is that "time in the saddle" is a non-negotiable element of experience. When moving from areas that are more practice-driven (such as sports or music) to careers (such as teaching or leading), it's more helpful to think in terms of years than hours. Having coached in various capacities for

---

[2] Check out, for instance, Tomasz Sacha:
https://youtu.be/nJysdWOWTc8

over twenty-five years, I just have a feel for it that no amount of studying can provide.

PERFECT PRACTICE MAKES PERFECT

One of my most impressive clients was a ten-year-old piano prodigy who was soon to be admitted to Julliard. As I was helping him prepare for media interviews and speeches, I often heard him say, "Practice doesn't make perfect—perfect practice makes perfect." It's not the first time I'd heard the quote but it's different coming from a ten-year-old who practices three hours a day with a surreal deliberateness.

The "Experience" section of your resume or LinkedIn profile might be an indicator of this Success Stave, but it might not. Just showing up for work year after year doesn't automatically mean you've mastered your craft. Mastery requires years of perfect and well-informed practice. I deliberately placed this chapter after the one on knowledge since experience can only be built on that foundation. Said another way, mastery is achieved by deliberately applying expertise over time.

Mastery is achieved by deliberately applying expertise over time.

THERE ARE NO NATURALS

Maybe a piano prodigy seems like an unhelpful example. "He's a natural," or "I can't compete with that," you might say. But there is no such thing as a "natural." No one slam dunks their first basketball or plays Liszt's Hungarian Rhapsody for their first recital. Instead, we all have personalities or talents that provide a *proclivity* toward something. That proclivity must be combined with practice for it to be of any value. My piano prodigy client has better hand-eye coordination than the majority of the population but without practice (and a lot of it) he could never have become an award-winning pianist with a bright future.

Practice plus proclivity equals a phenomenon; these are the rare few who not only had the talent but also put it to use and left an indelible mark on the world. Don't complain about not having that kind of proclivity—you can't control the amount of raw talents you've been given. What can you control? The amount of effort you put into the *practice* side of the equation—and that's the most important side. Practice without proclivity beats proclivity without practice. Practice's advantage over proclivity may not shine through immediately, but as the years increase, so will the gap between the two. Practice is patient work.

---

*Practice without proclivity beats
proclivity without practice.*

I said earlier that mastery is achieved by deliberately applying expertise over time. Here's what I mean by "deliberately": Where do you want to be successful? At the end of this chapter, there are some questions to help you find your "growth areas." I'll ask you to be as specific as you can. Maybe you need to become more proficient in Excel spreadsheets. Maybe you need to better understand social media (for marketing, not scrolling).

In my case, I realized early in my writing career that I lacked marketing knowledge and experience. Unlike bookkeeping, which I gladly outsource, successful authors know they must take point on their promotional efforts (unless their name is Stephen King). I enrolled in courses, read well-reviewed books, and talked to people who had proven themselves. Based on what I learned, I created a three-month plan that included various methods of promoting my book every day. As a result, it did better than I'd hoped, even showing up on the top of several "best books to read on public speaking" lists.

Here's my suggestion: Start by talking to those who both *know* and *do* better in your growth area. You don't know what you don't know, so ask what you need to learn and practice. Then, make your list and get to work. Learn, apply what you've learned, get feedback, apply the feedback, and keep going until you've reached your goal.

TAKE THE LONG VIEW

Experience cannot be faked. I guess you *could* fake a resume, but that's a really bad idea. More than that, it's incredibly short-sighted. Once discovered, the lie could have lifelong consequences. True success is all about the long game, making sacrifices now that will pay off later.

A great example of this is Kenny, a man who influenced me as a young leader. As the executive director of a small non-profit organization, he had many of the Success Drivers: well-educated, a gifted communicator, great with people, and very driven. His ambition was to lead a large non-profit organization, but his well-respected mentor told him, "You'll never get hired at that level unless you get some experience in a large organization." I'm sure that was some discouraging news and perhaps Kenny was tempted to lower his ambitions, but instead, he spent a year *volunteering* full time at a well-known large non-profit while his very supportive wife worked a second job to make ends meet. He's now the executive director at one of the fastest growing nonprofits in its sector. That's taking a long view!

INFORMAL PRACTICE

Maybe you read this chapter and feel like you've lost so much time or maybe it makes you second-guess a decision to switch careers—who wants to start their 10,000 hours all over? Be encouraged, you probably have more practice under your belt than you think because not all practice looks like practice.

Not all practice looks like practice.

Remember the movie The *Karate Kid*? Daniel-san doesn't know that all of Mr. Miyagi's chores were actually teaching him karate. As I said, you've likely put in far more of your 10,000 hours than you realize.

For example, my friend, who has written over a dozen books, was a pastor for years. When he started writing, he discovered that his weekly sermons had been developing his expertise and counted toward the 10,000.

Think about the things you've done and your interests. How do they apply to your field? Maybe your summer job taught you to work with multiple cultures or your time in Scouts developed resourcefulness. How can you retool these into relevant experience?

SELF-ASSESSMENT

Is your Experience Stave limiting your success?
Think both in terms of your mastery and what shows
up on the resume. Between the two, mastery is most
important, but your resume will determine what
doors are opened to you.

Identify some people who are considered successful in
your field. How does your education compare to theirs?

_____

_____

_____

How about your experience level?

_____

_____

_____

What are the steps you need to take to level up your
resume?

_____

_____

_____

Is taking those steps worth it to you? Why or why not?

_____

_____

_____

_____

Similar questions, but now focusing on mastery. Based on your field and personal definition of success, how would you define mastery?

_____

_____

_____

_____

If a novice is a 0 and a 10 is someone who has achieved mastery, what would you rank yourself? Why?

_____

_____

_____

_____

Now think in terms of the 10,000 hours/10 years. What percentage of those have you completed? Does that line up with your answer to the previous question? Why or why not?

_____

_____

_____

_____

_____

_____

_____

_____

Who are some people that merit a 10 ("Mastery")? What do they have that you don't?

_____

_____

_____

_____

_____

_____

_____

_____

What are some ways you can increase your real-life experience?

_____

_____

_____

_____

_____

Finally, let's take a look at the long road. Where would you like to be in ___ (you decide) years?

_____

_____

_____

_____

_____

With that in mind, what sacrifices are you willing to make now to gain the necessary experience?

_____

_____

_____

_____

_____

CHAPTER 3:

Communication

In my book, *Speak with No Fear*, I wrote that effective communication is a "universal advantage," a skill that gives you a leg up in just about every sector. This is true to an almost unfair extent. I've been observing a leader at a large organization for a while, and he's a phenomenal communicator, known on an international level. Because of his amazing communication, everyone assumes he's a great leader, but I have an inside source and know that he's not. More than anything, he's coasting on a silver tongue and his predecessor's success.

Leadership and communication go hand in hand. If you are great at leadership but can't communicate, people won't recognize your leadership, causing your influence (and hence leadership) to suffer. Conversely, if you're only a mediocre leader but strong in communication, you'll be better able to influence others and your leadership will be boosted.

Said another way, great communication improves leadership while weak communication diminishes it.

Great communication improves leadership while weak communication diminishes it.

See what I mean when I say it's almost an unfair advantage? The only reason it's "almost" is because *anyone* can become a better communicator. I've worked with hundreds of clients and have yet to meet an exception.

Communication doesn't necessarily mean speaking in front of crowds (but I believe anyone can learn that as well). It is the ability to 1) clearly convey your thoughts, beliefs, and feelings so they're understood by the hearer, and 2) accurately understand the thoughts, beliefs, and feelings of others, even if they struggle to express themselves.

Key examples include:

- Helping a client understand what you have to offer.
- Teaching a coworker how to perform a task.
- Encouraging a friend.
- Championing your cause or idea.

Of all five Success Drivers, I think more people are inclined to give themselves a pass on this one. They'll say things like:

"I'm not an extrovert."

- Many of the best speakers and communicators I know are introverts.

"English is not my first language."

- Neither was it Nelson Mandela's. Nor Mahatma Gandhi's. Nor Chimamanda Ngozi Adichie's. Nor Vladimir Nabokov's. Nor… and the list goes on.

"I don't like my voice/accent/laugh."

- It's part of what makes you you. Lean into it.

"I don't know how."

- Then it's time to learn.

"I'm neurodivergent and am incapable of interacting with people."

- You may have a tougher hill to climb, but there are plenty of other neurodivergent individuals who can prove you wrong.

Again, I've been coaching people for a long time so let me speak a hard truth. If you excuse yourself as a bad communicator, your success, your barrel's capacity, will always be limited by the Communication Stave.

Are there some bad communicators who were still successful? Sure. But, in every case, their knowledge and experience had to be extraordinary to make up for their poor communication. Imagine how much more successful they could have been had they been better communicators.

If you're serious about success, you cannot give yourself a pass on communication. I'm not saying you need to be a TEDx speaker, but you must strive to find your best. In fact, I'm frequently hired as a communication coach for people who aren't looking to be public speakers. They simply realize that it can take their medical practice, consultation services, or real estate business higher than ever before.

If you're serious about success, you cannot give yourself a pass on communication.

For some complimentary resources on public speaking, visit https://content.mikeacker.com or scan the QR code.

There you will find some short teachings that are the basis of effective public speaking.

THE 3-D'S OF COMMUNICATION

My latest book, *Speak with Confidence*, is the culmination of everything I've learned about public speaking, but almost all of it translates directly to general communication. It's beyond my scope here to repeat what I said there. My goal is giving you tools to assess yourself and map your journey to getting better.

These "3-D's" form the core of my coaching program:

1. Determine Your Identity

Even if the connection does not seem immediately obvious, years of experience have taught me that effective communication requires knowing who you are.

Imagine a teenager coming into the cafeteria at a new high school. If she doesn't know who she is, she'll look around for any table that will accept her. After sitting down, she'll observe the group and carefully answer questions about music and movies based on what she thinks everyone else wants to hear. Contrast that to the teenager who knows exactly who she is. She looks around to find her people and then heads straight for the table that fits her and confidently talks about her likes and dislikes. She listens to the other teens' opinions from a place of genuine interest instead of validation-seeking.

In the same way, you need to know yourself—your values, purpose, strengths, and weaknesses—to communicate with confidence.

- When you know your personal worth, you can speak your mind without worrying about rejection.
- When you know who you aren't, you will no longer need everyone to agree with you.
- When you know your values and life mission, you can speak about what matters to you.
- When you know what you do (and don't) know, you can teach the former and learn about the latter.
- When you know your strengths and weaknesses, you can build on the former and accommodate the latter.

I have my clients use various personality assessments and tools to understand themselves, but something this big requires more than a week's worth of introspection. Occasionally, they realize they need to unpack memories and experiences with a professional therapist—something I've done and occasionally still do with great benefit.

2. Define Your Message

Talking to some people is like listening to a politician answer a tricky question: they use a surprisingly large number of words to say nothing. Maybe it's because they're hiding the truth. Maybe they're hiding their ignorance. To communicate clearly, you must know your message with clarity. There are three elements to that.

Why: Have a Purpose

Whether we're talking about a book, speech, blog post, speaking up in a meeting, or sending an email, clear communication must have some sort of desperation. Why are you communicating it?

The Why drives the message. It creates the pathos—emotional impact—of Aristotle's three elements of persuasion (ethos and logos being the others). When you feel the message, you will communicate it with authority and passion, and your audience will feel it with you.

There are two levels to the Why.

Start with what the listener has to gain because that is where they start. People will only listen to you if it is to their benefit. What is your goal for the recipient? What are you hoping to do *for them*?

For instance, I want this book to take you to the next level, whether that's by motivating you to start a business, helping you gain a promotion, elevating your current influence, or some other way. The point is, if you are convinced that you have something of value to offer, then communicating it will take on a greater urgency; plus, it's more *fun*.

Second, what is the purpose for yourself? What are you hoping to gain? Speaking again about this book, my purpose vis-à-vis my coaching career is to extend my influence beyond the area of public speaking. By the way, knowing your identity helps you determine your why. Another aspect of this is having a personal and professional "identity statement" (as an added bonus, go to [identity.mikeacker.com] for a free PDF from my book, *The Identity Workbook*, which will begin to help you in creating a statement of your own).

What: Have a Point

This is obvious in theory but neglected in practice. Here is the rule of thumb I give my clients: If you can't effectively summarize your point in one to three sentences, then you either don't have one or don't understand the topic deeply enough. This holds true whether we're talking about a sales pitch, workshop, conference call, or speech.

Why is it so hard to pass the "summary test"? Lack of preparation is one reason, but too much is another. If you know a lot about your topic, your tendency will be to show off your knowledge. Either that or you'll hide behind it. What I mean is, if you don't know yourself and your value, you'll be tempted to overcompensate with a rush of words. As I pointed out in *Speak with Confidence*, "When we're talking, we feel like more words equal more authority. When we're listening, we think the opposite."

Here is what you need to understand: People don't want a perfect explanation; they want a good one. They won't remember all your points, but they can remember one point made with great clarity.

People don't want a perfect explanation, they want a good one.

Who: Understand the Audience

If there is no listener, there is no communication. If the listener doesn't understand, there is no communication. If the listener isn't interested, there is no communication. People are the reason for every talk you give and it's a privilege (not a duty) to be there. Our job, as communicators, is to serve the listeners, full stop. If you don't care about them, they'll know. You've probably heard it said, "People don't care how much you know, until they know how much you care." A lifetime of experience has proven the truth of this to me.

Additionally, you need to know who they are and what they need. I do not schedule a speech, workshop, or coaching session until I know enough about the audience to give them something of value in a way that connects with them.

3. Develop Your Skills

There's an element of art (and heart) to communication, but I prefer to think of it as a science, built on techniques that anyone can develop. Just like with any new skills, these aren't things you can magically pick up. Here's the process:

1. Become aware when something isn't working.

2. Learn a better skill.

3. Practice it "off stage."

4. Perform it "on stage."

Developing communication skills is a lifetime pursuit, but here are some key points that have benefited my clients the most:

- Pauses that invite input, create interest, and allow listeners to process what they've heard.

- Awareness of what posture says to the audience and how it affects you as the speaker.[3]

- Cadence, pacing, inflection, etc. and their ability to shape the sound of their message.

---

[3] See Amy Cuddy's TED Talk, "Your Body Language May Shape Who You Are."
https://www.ted.com/talks/amy_cuddy_your_body_language_may_shape_who_you_are

- The role of non-verbal communication.
- The importance of breathing.
- Controlling your verbal rabbit trails.
- Effective hand gestures.

HIGH COST OF LOW COMMUNICATION

How many movies or sitcom episodes revolve around a simple misunderstanding or poor communication? It's enjoyably aggravating to think, *Man! If they just would have talked to each other or said such and such, they could've avoided this whole mess.* Of course, there wouldn't be a plot if they had. But what's funny in a movie is devastating in real life. If you don't want your career turning into a soap opera, then you shouldn't ignore communication.

If you don't want your career turning into a soap opera, then you shouldn't ignore communication.

At the risk of repeating myself: no matter what you do, investing in better communication will propel you ahead and make up for any number of deficiencies. Barack Obama was young and relatively inexperienced. Ronald Reagan was an actor. Franklin D. Roosevelt was considered by some to be a "second-rate intellect." Abraham Lincoln was from the backwoods and lacked political connections. But all four were great communicators. Without that, they would not have made their mark on history.

SELF-ASSESSMENT

There are many types of communication. Some are interactive, like a back-and-forth conversation of some sort. Others are more one-sided, like writing an article or giving a speech. Strength in one type doesn't always equate to strength in another.

Assess your current ability in the key types below by asking questions such as:

- Do people typically understand what I'm trying to communicate?
- Do I enjoy this form of communication?
- How difficult is it for me to achieve good results?
- Do I understand the other party and their needs?

Emails, texts, and other interactive written communication:

Terrible ○ ○ ○ ○ ○ ○ ○ Exceptional

Blogs, articles, books, and other one-sided written communication:

Terrible ○ ○ ○ ○ ○ ○ ○ Exceptional

Personal conversations and "small talk":

Terrible ○ ○ ○ ○ ○ ○ ○ Exceptional

Business-related conversations:

Terrible ○ ○ ○ ○ ○ ○ ○ Exceptional

Explaining complicated matters effectively:

Terrible ○ ○ ○ ○ ○ ○ ○ Exceptional

High-conflict conversations:

Terrible ○ ○ ○ ○ ○ ○ ○ Exceptional

Making my voice heard in meetings:

Terrible ○ ○ ○ ○ ○ ○ ○ Exceptional

Speaking to small groups:

Terrible ○ ○ ○ ○ ○ ○ ○ Exceptional

Speaking to large groups:

Terrible ○ ○ ○ ○ ○ ○ ○ Exceptional

Listening and understanding others:

Terrible ○ ○ ○ ○ ○ ○ ○ Exceptional

(Note: Below, I left room for you to add types that apply to your situation.)

_____

Terrible ○ ○ ○ ○ ○ ○ ○ Exceptional

_____

Terrible ○ ○ ○ ○ ○ ○ ○ Exceptional

Not every one of these are equally important for every job. If you're in the tech department, the ability to explain things well and handle high conflict conversations are more crucial than speaking to large groups (though the latter could help you get that promotion).

Go back through the list above and star the types most crucial for your success and then notice how you've assessed yourself on those. What does this tell you about your relative ability in that area of communication? How is this affecting your success?

_____

_____

_____

_____

_____

Based on what you learned, what are some steps you can take to build up this Success Stave?

_____

_____

_____

_____

_____

_____

BEYOND THE RESUME

Before we move on to the final two Success Drivers, I want to point out something very important about knowledge, experience, and communication.

In the preindustrial world, most people were born, lived, and died in the same village. You'd most likely work in your family's profession or be apprenticed to someone in town. There wasn't anything like the modern interview process because everyone already knew you. Knowledge and experience took a back seat to character because those can be taught but character cannot.

These days, we have far more mobility and greater opportunities, which means that you'll almost certainly be hired by someone who doesn't know you. In a system driven by resumes, knowledge and experience are in the front seat and companies hope that candidates have the character to go with it.

I've had the privilege of working with some highly skilled executives, some of whom are experts in hiring, and they helped me understand why the resume and interview system has such a high failure rate—and why you must move beyond the first three Success Drivers.

Knowledge and experience may get you the interview, so your tendency will be to give them a disproportional amount of energy. Communication is invaluable once you get to the interview, but it is also limited. Many people have talked their way into a position they weren't equipped for. Others haven't gotten a position they were highly qualified for simply because of poor communication skills. Accordingly, I believe it's the Success Staves of emotional intelligence and drive that will keep you in a position and also allow you to thrive there. Without them, your capacity for success will be far below what it should be.

My point? Don't stop reading now.

CHAPTER 4:

Emotional Intelligence

Think about the healthiest, most enjoyable places you've worked at. Then, think about the most toxic. Even if you can't write out a dictionary definition of emotional intelligence, you intuitively understand that some people are more emotionally healthy than others and that, more than any other factor, impacts workplace atmosphere.

Emotional intelligence (EI) is the ability to make sound judgments about your emotions and those of others, then choose the wisest course of action (which is seldom the same thing as the most gratifying). In my book, *Connect Through Emotional Intelligence*, I use the analogy of taking a road trip with a group of friends, each driving their own car. EI represents:

    1.   Understanding and controlling your "car" (emotional state).

2. Being able to read and safely interact with the other cars on the road (people in general).

3. Working in a productive manner with the other cars in your group, allowing everyone to arrive at the shared destination.

Far from being a "touchy-feely" concept, EI is consistently a better predictor of success than IQ. It's hard to get anywhere if you keep crashing your car into every obstacle and all the other cars around you. Having the ability to handle adversity, understand yourself, and connect with others will radically increase your potential for success. Lacking those abilities is a significant Success Limiter—if you wouldn't want to work with someone like you, do you think anyone else would either?

GAUGING YOUR EI

There are many resources for evaluating your EI that are well worth using, but you can start with questions like these:

- Can you recognize what you are feeling, and why, at any given time?
- Are you able to reach beyond the surface "why" and determine the root causes?

- How long does it take you to recover from distressing emotions?
- Can you sense how other people are feeling and understand their points of view?
- What sort of effect do you have on the people you work with?

Just as with the natural proclivities discussed in Chapter 2, some people seem to have a natural advantage here. Things like your childhood, personal temperament, and life experiences can significantly impact your EI, but *everyone* can increase theirs. And there's another dynamic I've noticed: Many of the things that ostensibly cause a lower EI can be converted into a higher EI when acknowledged and healed. For instance, someone who grew up in an emotionally abusive household may have a greater capacity for empathy than someone who had a relatively trouble-free childhood.

One more thing: Beware of confusing EI with specific personality types or being a nice person. There are plenty of nice people who aren't emotionally healthy (e.g., people pleasers) as well as straight shooters who are.

NON-NEGOTIABLE

Developing a high EI cannot be done via an online quiz, a handful of inspirational quotes, or reading a stack of books. It's an ongoing journey, filled with ever deepening revelations and newfound understandings. The most important thing I can do is convince you that it is necessary and that it is possible.

If you have enough emotional intelligence, and have worked with people who don't, then there's no need to convince you of the necessary part. If, on the other hand, you think EI is a stupid fad, I'd encourage you to look back on your life. Does it resemble the Demotivator poster from the 90s that reads, "The only consistent feature of all of your dissatisfying relationships is you"? That may seem harsh, but the people with the lowest EI are consistently the ones most blinded to the fact.

Or maybe you know your EI needs work, but it feels hopeless. As with communication, I've never met anyone who cannot improve their emotional health—providing they're willing to do the work. You may not become the next Brene Brown, but you will find your happiness and wellbeing increase, along with your external success.

THREE KEYS TO EI

As with every one of the five Success Drivers, there is far more that can be said than I have room to say. Instead, I want to give you what I believe to be the three most helpful keys to EI:

1. Self-focus

Not *being* self-focused but self-focus. This starts with a sense of identity and self-worth, as covered in Chapter 3, then moves to things like:

- Self-understanding
- Self-awareness
- Self-control
- Self-regulation
- Self-motivation

Have you ever started driving a rental car without familiarizing yourself with all the buttons, knobs, and features? My first experience with "driver's assist" happened in a rental car as I was speeding down an interstate. Suddenly, the car started doing some weird stuff, which was a little freaky. But it was acting exactly as it should, protecting me from drifting into another lane.

In the same way, if you don't understand yourself and aren't aware of how your psyche handles various stimuli, it's easy to feel out of control. Developing EI requires you to understand what's happening inside of you and why, which allows you to get back into the driver's seat. Regulating yourself doesn't mean going all Spock and being emotionless. Instead, it is about directing your emotions and expressing them in appropriate ways, at appropriate times.

As you gain awareness and control of what's happening inside you, it transforms how you respond to what happens *outside* you. I've written elsewhere about the fundamental principle of "loci of control." Do you believe that life happens to you and you are a victim of it (external locus of control)? Or that you can affect change and are responsible for your own choices (internal locus of control)?

The difference between saying, "She made me mad!" and "I got mad" is more than semantics. If someone "makes you" mad, you have no control over yourself and any attempt to change is pointless. If you "got" mad, then you can ask why and how you can prevent it next time. EI is built upon understanding and taking ownership of your emotional state.

Just this one example of "She made me mad!" has so many implications in the workplace. Think of any customer service position. You have to deal with a lot of people who have unbelievably low EI. It doesn't matter if you're a waitress, salesperson, or tech support. If you are constantly allowing others to drive your emotional state, you'll never be successful.

2. Others-attunement

Ironically, it's only when you have self-focus that you can be others-attuned. That's because your attention shifts from "How are you affecting me?" to "How are you feeling?" When you are no longer thinking about them in relation to yourself but instead recognize them as free moral agents who have their own emotions, then you can explore those feelings with curiosity instead of defensiveness and judgment. This is all about building an empathetic connection—treating and accepting others as real people.

One great tool for fostering empathy through conversation is the ALAER approach. I discovered it years ago and use it regularly:

- **A**sk questions: Thoughtful questions both demonstrate interest and invite honest responses.

- **L**isten actively: This involves attending to both verbal and non-verbal communication. Instead of mentally preparing your response, demonstrate that you are listening through posture and clarifying questions.

- **A**cknowledge the heart: More than responding to the "what," listen for and affirm the "why," which is typically deeper than facts.

- **E**xplore with curiosity: Knowing their "why" puts you in the position to both empathize and ask more questions that help you (and them) better understand the situation.

- **R**espond appropriately: It may take a couple times through the first four steps, but once you really understand, you'll be able to respond without making assumptions about the situation or their motivations.

People seldomly understand what is happening in their hearts and the ALAER approach will allow you to help them discover it. You may find that what seemed like an insurmountable problem was actually a simple misunderstanding.

3. Social Skills

How are you at remembering names? Just about everyone claims to be bad at it, but the reality is most don't really try. If I were to send you into a crowded room and offer $100 for every person you could name the following day, you'd quickly become an expert on name-memorization techniques! Remembering names is just one of many skills you can develop to exponentially improve your EI.

Examples include:

- Having a collection of "connection questions" when meeting someone new, such as asking for some personal trivia or where they've traveled.

- Developing an interest in other people's interests.
- Practicing appropriate eye contact (different cultures define this differently, so do your homework).
- Learning to read the emotional temperature in a room.
- Studying the difference between Passive, Aggressive, Passive-Aggressive, and Assertive communication and training yourself to only use the latter.
- Keeping your cell phone silenced and tucked away during conversations.

There is so much more that can be said here. Dale Carnegie's *How to Win Friends and Influence People* is one of the most practical sources I can think of for more examples. But it all comes down to the Golden Rule: Do unto others as you would have them do unto you.

CONFLICT, CRITICISM, AND CRITICISM

If self-focus, others-attunement, and social skills are three of the most helpful keys to emotional intelligence then conflict, criticism, and criticism are three of the most important opportunities to apply

EI. Yes, I named "criticism" twice—one for receiving it and one for giving it.

1. Conflict

Conflict, while unpleasant, is not inherently bad. It is, in fact, crucial for breaking past surface interactions. Additionally, some of the worst examples of leadership stem from conflict avoidance. Don't believe me? Just watch a season of *The Office*. Half of Michael Scott's problems stem from his unwillingness to engage in productive conflict. If you're a Michael Scott who tolerates poor results or allows toxic behaviors to go unchecked (or a Dwight Schrute who enjoys conflict!) do your career and your coworkers a favor and invest in studying healthy conflict.

The three keys above are key to handling conflict in a productive manner. *Self-focus* includes a healthy sense of self-worth that doesn't avoid conflict for fear of being disliked (which, as we see in Michael Scott's case, usually makes people like you even less). *Others-attunement* allows you to understand the other person's perspective without judgment and respond with empathy. *Social skills* represent the numerous tools you can gather for productive conflict resolution.

2. Benefiting from Criticism

Similarly, a strong sense of self allows you to separate your personal value from the thing which is being critiqued. When receiving criticism, the question moves from, "Am I a worthwhile person?" to "Is this useful?" Notice that the critic's motives and/or delivery method becomes irrelevant. I've received some book reviews that were nasty and driven by the reviewer's desire to be clever but, because I didn't need their approval, I was still able to gain benefit from them.

3. Giving Helpful Criticism

I once heard a pastor say, "God loves you just the way you are but too much to leave you there." In the same way, delivering vital "hard feedback" can be an act of kindness and withholding it, an act of selfishness (i.e., caring more about your fear of conflict than their need to grow).

Again, this requires both a healthy self-worth and others-attunement. But good intentions are not enough. Social skills are vital for delivering criticism in a manner most likely to communicate your concern and be well received. One useful technique, for example, is the "compliment sandwich," which involves sandwiching hard feedback between two compliments. However, this only works if you're already in the habit of complimenting people outside of these conversations. A good rule of thumb is maintaining a ratio of seven compliments or positive actions for every one piece of critical feedback.

SELF-ASSESSMENT

Perhaps emotional intelligence is the most difficult of the Success Limiters to assess. Very few people can understand how other people see them! There are many online assessments available, so I encourage you to take several of them before proceeding (don't rely on just one or two).

Given what you've discovered, where is one area you show a high EI?

_____

_____

_____

Where is one area you showed a low EI?

_____

_____

_____

How do you think your EI has negatively impacted your success?

_____

_____

_____

How would you rate your self-focus and why?

Poor ○ ○ ○ ○ ○ ○ ○ Great

_____

_____

_____

_____

How would you rate your others-attunement and why?

Poor ○ ○ ○ ○ ○ ○ ○ Great

_____

_____

_____

_____

What are some social skills you want to develop?

_____

_____

_____

_____

_____

_____

_____

In some of the following questions, you'll notice I don't give a "right" choice. Instead, I want you to consider which unhealthy extreme you are most inclined to and to what degree.

How would you describe the way you respond to conflict?

Avoid at all costs ○ ○ ○ ○ ○ ○ ○ Always ready for a fight

How do you *wish* you responded to conflict?

_____

_____

_____

_____

Of the three keys (self-focus, others-attunement, and social skills), which one could best improve your response to conflict? What steps do you want to take to get there?

How do you typically respond to critique and criticism?

Devastation ○ ○ ○ ○ ○ ○ ○ Defiance

_____

_____

_____

How do you want to grow in this area?

_____

_____

_____

_____

How do you typically handle giving critiques?

| All kindness, no truth | ○ | ○ | ○ | ○ | ○ | ○ | ○ | All truth, no kindness |

Of the three keys, which one could best improve how you give hard feedback? What's your plan?

_____

_____

_____

_____

Review your answers above. Prioritize your top three "next steps" for improving your EI.

_____

_____

_____

_____

CHAPTER 5:

Drive

The final Success Stave is drive; it is the vital, but hard-to-quantify, question of, "How badly do you want it?"

I was tempted to find a different word than "drive" for this one but decided I like the repetition. Drive is what drives all the other drivers to success—driveless drivers can't drive you anywhere. What I mean is, if you have knowledge, experience, communication, and EI, but don't do anything with it, nothing's going to happen. Back to the whiskey barrel, if this stave is missing, it doesn't matter how high the others are. But if you have drive, you'll get the full use out of the other four.

Said another way, drive is the great equalizer. It's available to everyone. It is not based on DNA, geography, or family of origin but only by the choices you make. In fact, having the four other Success Staves can actually work *against* you when it comes to drive. The person with the other four can be prone to complacency and coasting on past success. But the underdog has nothing to lose and everything to prove.

Drive is the great equalizer.

I've discovered that drive has three elements. I say "elements," but they're really more like steps, each one building on the prior.

1. Goals

All the effort in the world is wasted if it isn't channeled. Not only does a goal provide focus, but it also brings clarity. How can you know you're successful without a metric by which to define it? To be effective, goals…

…need to be specific.

JFK's famous "Moon" speech worked for many reasons, one of which is it gave a specific goal (man on the moon) with a clear deadline (end of the decade).

…need to be ABBA—Audacious But (Barely) Achievable.

Push yourself to go further than you think possible but don't set a goal that's pure fantasy or, worse yet, disheartening.

…need to be recorded.

I was going to retell the famous Harvard/Yale study of the increased effectiveness of written goals, but it turns out it may be an urban legend. Regardless, experience has taught me that goals that get written, get done. Not only does it create a sense of commitment, but the writing process also brings clarity.

…need to have a plan.

A goal without a plan is a daydream. Creating a plan not only gives you an achievable process, but it also gets you moving. Planning isn't a substitute for action, but it's a good start.

A goal without a plan is a daydream.

---

2. Motivation

Any audacious goal will require a massive investment on your part. You may need to kiss social media and Netflix-binging goodbye. You may not be home at 5:30 every night. You may have to spend money without a clear promise of payback. With each sacrifice, you'll be tempted to quit. For this reason, you'll need a clear motivation propelling you forward.

In his book, *The Compound Effect*, Darren Hardy gives the following illustration: If someone offers you $20 to walk across a plank in a parking lot, you'd probably go for it. The reward isn't huge, but neither is the risk. If, however, that plank was resting between two high-rises, $20 wouldn't be remotely enough. But what if the other building was on fire and your child was trapped inside? Would you walk across to save him/her? The risk hasn't changed but the reward has increased by a factor of one trillion.

The bigger the risk and higher the cost of your goal, the greater the motivation must be. For the *really* big goals, money and fame will not be enough. You will need something deeper. And, if you think about it, money and fame are just means to some other end, be it security, identity, happiness, or a chance to change the world.

Dig deeper, beneath the surface motivations, and answer this question with clarity: Why does this matter to you? If you can't answer that, you won't have a chance of developing the final element of drive.

3. Grit

Grit is nothing more than the daily choice to keep going, even when you don't want to. It doesn't matter if you're trying to do something as trivial as getting out of bed for the gym or something as monumental as spending your entire life fighting racism, grit is non-negotiable. No one gets to the top of the mountain without climbing through a lot of mud. It's when you want to give up that you discover what you are made of and how much it really means to you.

No one gets to the top of the mountain
without climbing through a lot of mud.

Starting is exciting. You have a big goal and it's a little scary, but you're inspired and ready to take on the world. That will last you for a while, but (sooner or later) it's going to get hard. Or you'll face setbacks. Or you'll get bored and something shiny will compete for your attention. Whatever the case, you just won't be feeling inspired anymore:

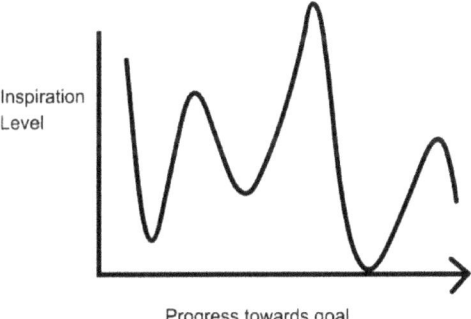

Progress towards goal

Grit is what takes over when pursuing your goal isn't fun. Grit keeps you going when your motivation is no longer inspiring. Grit is continually choosing the long-term good over the immediate gratification.

There aren't any magic tricks that provide instant grit, but there are some great tools for developing it over time:

- Journaling your "why."
- Charting your progress.
- Listening to motivating podcasts.
- Developing other good habits (discipline in one area breeds discipline in others).
- Creating routines that allow habits to take over when desire fades.
- Asking friends to keep you accountable.
- Posting updates on social media.

Contrary to how it feels, it's when your desire tapers off and your grit kicks in that you experience the most internal growth and make the greatest progress toward your goal.

DRIVEN TO WRITE

When I was in my mid-twenties, I wrote the first draft of a book I wasn't able to get over the finish line. When I couldn't find a publisher, discouragement and frustration took over and I left it sitting forgotten in my hard drive.

Years later, when my coaching practice was growing but was still more of a hobby than a business, I started working with Rachel, a very successful self-published author. I helped her become a better speaker while she showed me that I could be published without following the usual route. As I learned more about her process and realized she was just a normal person, like me (and younger too), my old daydream of writing a book seemed possible. I found the question, *What if…? What if…?* running through my mind.

What if I could be successful without a traditional publisher?

What if I could impact people the way Rachel had?

What if I could use a book to turn my coaching hobby into a career?

What if I could become a thought leader in the field of public speaking?

No longer limited by the "impossibility" of being published, I was motivated to realize my potential. Wanting to discover what I was capable of, I began educating myself. I read books about writing. I listened to podcasts. I talked to other authors and joined Chandler Bolt's Self-Publishing School. This education was absolutely vital (and the lack thereof was probably the reason for my first book's failure). But I also gave myself a limited amount of time for education because many would-be authors never get past this phase—there's always more to learn and learning is less scary than writing.

Next, I set an audacious goal to get me moving: Write a book in 30 days (they do it for NaNoWriMo,[4] right?) and publish it within 90. When I journaled my goal, it became much more real. And once I posted it on social media and started receiving all sorts of "You can do it!" messages, I was committed.

That was my goal. What was my motivation? On the surface, it was not wasting the few thousand dollars I spent on Self-Publishing School—spending money is a great way to drive yourself forward! But deeper than that was answering all my "what if?" questions.

High on inspiration, I woke up at 4:45 on Day 1, took a cold shower, brewed a cup of coffee, and wrote from 5:00-6:00. After that, I went through my normal routine: coaching appointments, followed by my "day job," and time with my family. I wrote some more that night, went to bed, and started all over again the next day. By Day 14, I was exhausted, could barely remember what I was doing, and definitely wasn't feeling inspired. That was when the habits I'd built over the previous two weeks became vital. It was nothing but grit that got me through the next week and a half. Then, the finish line came into view, and I sprinted to the end, completing the rough draft on Day 27. It had been brutal, but I was done. Time to celebrate!

---

[4] A.k.a. National Novel Writing Month, https://nanowrimo.org/.

Or so I thought…

Knowing my book wasn't perfect, I sent it to Rachel for "some" editing. My precious book came back torn apart and covered in red ink. After all the hours of writing and countless sacrifices I'd made, it was a real kick in the gut. The thought of going through *that* again was unbearable. I began to doubt myself—who was I to write a book? What did I have to say? But I kept returning to a comment she'd made, "Mike, this is going to help so many people." That was what I needed to hear. I spent another month editing and then another formatting, designing, and preparing it. On May 22nd, 2019, 87 days after my first 5:00 a.m. session, I published my first book.

It was grit that got me through the 5:00 a.m. writing. It was grit that got me through all my doubt. It was grit that brought me a book that sold far better than I'd hoped (and has indeed helped so many people) and launched me into full-time speaking and coaching.

Was it always fun? No.

Was it worth it? Absolutely, and that's what grit is all about.

LUCK - THE SIXTH STAVE?

Do you have a friend who is always lucky? They just happen to meet the right person who just happens to mention a dream opportunity. And then they just happened to read an online article that leads to a connection that gives them the chance to meet their hero. And then they happened to get a new client that flies them to Africa. And then…

Jay is *that* friend of mine. I'd mentored him a couple years back and we got together for lunch to catch up. He regaled me with stories of incredible deals on a house, RV, and several vehicles that he'd resold for a significant profit. He continued with the trips, unexpected opportunities, and business ventures he'd landed. Just when I was about to get jealous of hearing about all his luck, he paused and said, "You know, people always tell me how lucky I am, but I've found that luck is just hard work."

Jay was unintentionally paraphrasing the great Roman philosopher, Seneca:

"Luck is what happens when preparation meets opportunity."

Without a doubt, being successful almost always includes a certain element of luck—meeting the right person, overhearing a conversation, or any number of coincidences—so much so that luck could almost be considered the sixth Success Stave.

This may seem unfair until you realize that luck and fate are not the same thing. Fate implies a hopeless absence of personal agency but, with luck, you can radically increase your odds. It's like the difference between a single round of one card draw and a Texas hold 'em tournament. You can't control the cards you're dealt in either game, but skill and strategy can win hold' em over the long run. Said another way, the "opportunity" side of Seneca's equation is out of your hands, but the "preparation" side isn't.

This takes us right back to the Drive Stave. In the famous words of legendary Hollywood producer, Samuel Goldwyn (the "G" in MGM Pictures):

"The harder I work, the luckier I get."

You can't make luck happen, but drive makes work happen, and that is close enough.

You can't make luck happen, but drive makes work happen, and that is close enough.

SELF-ASSESSMENT

Think back through your life. When was a time you demonstrated great drive, maintaining maximum effort over the long haul?

_____

_____

_____

_____

Likewise, when was a time that your lack of drive cost you something you really wanted?

_____

_____

_____

_____

_____

_____

_____

Now rate the quality of your goal, motivation, and grit during the above episodes (use a check for the first one and "x" for the second):

The importance of the goal:

| Forgett-able | ○ | ○ | ○ | ○ | ○ | ○ | ○ | Literally Life-changing |

The inspiration of your motivation:

| Trivial | ○ | ○ | ○ | ○ | ○ | ○ | ○ | Life or Death |

The depth of your grit:

| Backyard Puddle | ○ | ○ | ○ | ○ | ○ | ○ | ○ | Mariana Trench |

Examine your answers. How have goals, motivation, and grit affected your drive? Which of the three had the greatest impact?

_____

_____

_____

_____

_____

_____

Of the tools I offered for increasing grit, which two do you think would be most useful for you?

_____

_____

_____

_____

_____

Do you consider yourself lucky? Why or why not?

_____

_____

_____

_____

_____

If your dream opportunity were to present itself, how prepared would you be for it?

_____

_____

_____

_____

_____

_____

CHAPTER 6:

Next Steps

Over the course of this book, we've looked at the five drivers of success, specifically as they relate to career building. Not surprisingly, they're equally applicable to many other areas of life. For example, if your marriage isn't as meaningful as you'd like, you could retool the Success Drivers like this:

- Knowledge

  What do you need to learn about marriage? About your spouse? About yourself? Are there some books you could purchase? Could counseling give you the information you need?

- Experience

  Newlyweds cannot expect to have the same level of depth as a couple celebrating 50 years together, but "perfect practice makes perfect." Years of treading water doesn't count for nearly as much as intentionally moving forward.

- Communication

  Do I even need to say this? Developing communication skills will have a massive positive impact on all your relationships.

- Emotional Intelligence

  Raising your EI, especially as it relates to empathy and conflict resolution, will allow you to love and understand your spouse better and set you up to receive their love in healthier ways.

- Drive

  Romance is the "feeling inspired" phase of marriage. It's lots of fun but won't get you through the normal challenges and when inspiration runs low (never mind when tragedies strike).

To find success in marriage, ask yourself which of these is your biggest Success Limiter and focus on *that* one—all the marriage books in the world won't help if you only communicate in grunts.

Don't neglect the value of this model for finding success in every area of your life: parenting, fitness, spiritual growth, getting your finances under control, and so on. In fact, success in *these* areas frequently offer greater life satisfaction than your career ever could. I'll leave it to you to think about how that applies to you.

Changing Seasons

I started this book by asking, "What's limiting you?" As you've been reading and answering the questions, you probably have a clear idea of your shortest Success Stave. You may have also noticed that your answer has changed throughout the years.

My career in full-time NGO work started when I was twenty-two. I had a newly minted degree, better than average communication skills, and reasonably high EI. Experience was undoubtedly my main Success Limiter, but I was very driven and desperate to prove myself. Being single allowed me to pour all my energy into work. I spent my off-hours reading, going to seminars, and interviewing leaders in my field—even driving thirty-two hours cross-country to meet one. I also chose positions based not on the salary they offered but the experience I'd gain and impact I could make. It worked. I went from influencing a little group of ten to crowds of 10,000 and, within my network, I was seen as an up-and-coming leader.

When I got married at age thirty, I had to adjust my priorities and seek more success in marriage than business. The birth of our son required even more adjustments. After that, I transitioned into corporate work. Even though I was new to that sector, a lot of my experience carried over, allowing me to start at six-figures. Likewise, my communication skills, EI, and drive all benefited me there. Suddenly, knowledge was my shortest Success Stave, and I went into overtime to bring it up. Then, after *Speak with No Fear* came out, I transitioned into being a communication coach/entrepreneur and my salary quickly doubled and even tripled from what I made in the corporate world.

What's my shortest stave now?

Drive. I know I could be making more money than I am, but it's for good reason. My son is seven and I only have a couple more years of being as "hands on" as I get to be now, so I'm driven to build a fantastic relationship with him. Being an entrepreneur gives me the flexibility to drop my son off for school, pick him up in the afternoons, and attend most of his events—sometimes the only dad in attendance. Even though my work often takes me out of town, I've been able to build a tighter relationship with my wife and son than ever before and that's worth some missed opportunities.

Again, this is a conscious choice and I'm aware it's costing me some professional success in this phase of my life, but my career is not (and will never be) my highest priority. In a few years, when Paxton gets older, it will be time to make some changes and focus again on my Drive Stave.

YOUR TURN

As I said earlier, if you picked up this book, it probably means you aren't happy with the current level of your barrel and want to level up. If you've gotten this far, it means you really want to do something about it.

Congratulations.

I mean it—many people would stop reading when they get to something uncomfortable (like being told they have to improve their Communication Stave).

Without diagnosing the reason (i.e., which Success Limiter is at fault), what led you to read this book? What is missing in your career or life that you want to change?

_____

_____

_____

_____

_____

_____

_____

Using this diagram, mark where you believe each of your Success Staves are currently at.

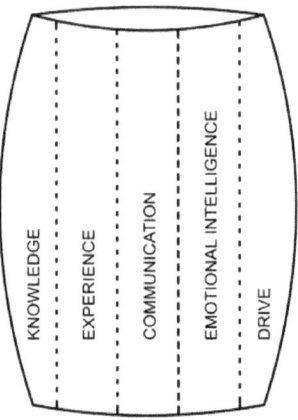

Study this for a moment and visualize your potential for success leaking out. How important is fixing your barrel to you? Why is now the time?

_____

_____

_____

_____

_____

_____

_____

Based on what you've discovered, what are the first and second most important Success Staves for you to fix?

_____

_____

_____

_____

_____

_____

_____

_____

Now brainstorm 15-20 tactics for doing so. No self-editing—the only bad idea is one you don't write down.

_____

_____

_____

_____

_____

_____

_____

_____

_____

Go through the above list and pick the top three (per driver), then prioritize them based upon what will fix your barrel the quickest.

Finally, create a plan for each of your top six tactics.

_____

_____

_____

_____

_____

_____

_____

_____

_____

_____

_____

_____

_____

_____

_____

_____

_____

_____

THAT'S EASY FOR YOU TO SAY...

This book is only the beginning of a much longer journey. Each Success Driver can and does have whole books written about them. But just as important as the drivers, are the obstacles you'll face when trying to apply everything I've said. In *Speak with Confidence*, I devoted two chapters to overcoming several obstacles such as:

- Imposter syndrome
- Victim mentality
- Limiting beliefs
- Comparisons
- Rejection

Most of these obstacles can be summed up by the objection, "That's easy for you to say, Mike. But…" and insert the excuse here.

Sure, I've had some advantages going in, but I've also had many disadvantages, including a speech impediment. Let's be honest, there are thousands of stories about people who've picked themselves up from worse. Comparison is always a losing game. So, as an encouragement (and not a comparison), I want to close with an example from someone whose drive has inspired me and pushed me further—my big sister and total badass, Ayanna Mostofi.

Ayanna and I both share the challenges and advantages of growing up in Mazatlán, Mexico with parents who ran an NGO in an economically challenged area. We also shared the advantage of a mom and dad who loved us, believed in us, and pushed us to excel academically—but not at the expense of our personal or spiritual well-being. Through everyday events, like hosting supporters, they actively developed our emotional intelligence and communication skills.

My sister, however, didn't have the chance to attend college. She got married at eighteen and had three children by the age at which I started my career. Her husband worked long hours, so her main focus was success in parenting, and she pursued it with everything she had—reading books, finding mentors, and practicing everything she learned. As her kids entered school, she decided to build a career in real estate by going back to school, getting her license, and finding new mentors. Then came the twins, followed by another child.

That was when the recession hit and the market collapsed. People were getting out of real estate left and right, but she dove in even more. While her older kids were in class, she'd pack up the younger ones and drive all around western Washington as they napped, finding the opportunities others missed. Even as a busy mom, she would use early mornings, school hours, and late evenings to build her business. She tried so many different things, some that failed but many that succeeded. Now, after twenty-five years of marriage, she is doing extremely well for herself and can enjoy the benefits of her and her husband's hard work: a lake house, a home in a resort community, nice vacations, etc. But she's hardly coasting. My sister continues to set ambitious goals and works beyond tired. I say "beyond tired" instead of "tirelessly" because she does get tired—but keeps working anyway.

I wonder how many people dismissed Ayanna as another "teenage mother" and said things like, "She had such potential…" I wonder how often she felt like she'd missed her opportunity. But instead of falling into despair, the obstacles motivated her to work harder and push herself further. It's that drive that now inspires me to do the same, and I'm grateful for her example.

YOUR BEST

In her classic children's story, *A Wrinkle in Time*, Madeleine L'Engle says, "Like and equal are not the same thing at all." I firmly believe that we are all children of God and are equally valuable, but we are not at all alike. You may have some real limitations and disadvantages that others don't. Then again, you probably have some unique advantages as well. Neither of those matter. I believe we are best judged not on a curve against others nor by our total "output." Instead, the question is, "What did you do with what you were given?" The goal of this book has been to help you find your greatest possible success, the total possible capacity of your barrel.

The question is, "What did you do with what you were given?"

My hope is that I've helped you discover your Success Limiters, those areas that are holding you back from being the best version of you, and provided the tools to mend your barrel. But none of it will help if you don't get started. Earlier in this chapter, I had you write six different strategies for increasing your success, but if you're feeling a little overwhelmed, I want to make it a little easier. Just do the first "next thing."

That's it.

Take one step and the others will follow, but it starts with one step.

FOR FURTHER STUDY

GENERAL BOOKS

The 15 Invaluable Laws of Growth: Live Them and Reach Your Potential, by John Maxwell.

Talent Is Never Enough: Discover the Choices That Will Take You Beyond Your Talent, by John Maxwell.

KNOWLEDGE

In addition to studying your specific field (via books, trade journals, podcasts, etc.), "cross-disciplinary" reading can often result in unexpected insights. Memoirs are great resources as well as popular books by experts in other fields, e.g., *A Brief History of Time* (Stephen Hawking) and *Freakonomics* (Steven D. Levitt and Stephen J. Dubner).

The Complete Idiot's Guide to Speed Reading by Abby Marks Beale.

Sometimes You Win--Sometimes You Learn: Life's Greatest Lessons Are Gained from Our Losses by John Maxwell.

How to Read a Book: The Classic Guide to Intelligent Reading Paperback by Mortimer J. Adler and Charles Van Doren.

Mastery by Robert Green.

EXPERIENCE

Atomic Habits by James Clear.

The 21 Irrefutable Laws of Leadership: Follow Them and People Will Follow You by John Maxwell.

Outliers by Malcom Gladwell.

Principles by Ray Dalio.

COMMUNICATION

Talk Like TED: The 9 Public-Speaking Secrets of the World's Top Minds Paperback by Carmine Gallo.

Speak & Meet Virtually: Go from Zoom Fatigue, Online Meeting Boredom, and Impersonal Presentations to Engaging, Efficient, and Empowering Web Conferencing by Mike Acker.

Speak with Confidence: Overcome Self-Doubt, Communicate Clearly, and Inspire Your Audience by Mike Acker.

Speak with No Fear: Go from a Nervous, Nauseated, and Sweaty Speaker to an Excited, Energized, and Passionate Presenter by Mike Acker.

The Art of Public Speaking by Stephen Lucas.

Unleash the Power of Storytelling: Win Hearts, Change Minds, Get Results by Rob Biesenbach.

EMOTIONAL INTELLIGENCE

How to Win Friends & Influence People by Dale Carnegie.

Emotional Intelligence 2.0 by Daniel Goleman.

Crucial Conversations: Tools for Talking When Stakes are High, Third Edition by Joseph Grenny and Kerry Patterson, et al.

Connect through Emotional Intelligence: Learn to master self, understand others, and build strong, productive relationships by Mike Acker.

Lead with No Fear by Steve Gutzler and Mike Acker.

Relational Intelligence by Steve Saccone.

DRIVE

Grit: The Power of Passion and Perseverance by Angela Duckworth.

Can't Hurt Me: Master Your Mind and Defy the Odds by David Goggins.

Failing Forward: Turning Mistakes into Stepping Stones for Success by John Maxwell.

Grow Your Soul: A 40-Day Guide to Get Unstuck, Restored, and Reset in Faith, Church, and Spirit by Mike Acker.

The Identity Workbook: Discover, Define, and Determine a Statement That Reflects Who You Are to Guide You in What You Do and How You Live by Mike Acker.

ABOUT MIKE ACKER

Mike Acker is a keynote speaker, author, executive, and communication coach with over twenty years of speaking, leadership development, and organizational management experience.

Beyond corporate training, Mike engages in his community as a Seattle TEDx speaker coach and works with international agencies to provide relief amidst poverty.

Mike also enjoys rock-climbing, wake surfing, skiing, church, building Legos with his son, Paxton, and going on dates with his wife, Taylor. Mike believes in the power of prayer, exercise, journaling, and real community to counter the stresses of everyday life.

http://www.mikeacker.com

www.ingramcontent.com/pod-product-compliance
Lightning Source LLC
Chambersburg PA
CBHW051542120626
46551CB00013B/1340